The End of Me
By Megan Morgan
Published 2019 by Your Book Angel
Copyright © Megan Morgan

All rights reserved. No part of this publication may be reproduced, stored in or introduced into a retrieval system, or transmitted in any form, or by any means (electronic, mechanical, photocopying, recording, or otherwise) without the prior written consent of the publisher.

This book is sold subject to the condition that it shall not, by way of trade or otherwise, be resold, hired out, or otherwise circulated without the publisher's prior consent in any form of binding or cover other than that in which it is published and without a similar condition including this condition being imposed on the subsequent purchaser.

Printed in the United States

Edited by Keidi Keating

Layout by Christi Koehl

ISBN: 978-1-7335939-0-8

The End of Me

By Megan Morgan

*For Richard, Sandelle and Jesha - for always believing
in me, even when I didn't, couldn't or wouldn't,
for loving me fiercely despite all the ups and downs.
I love you and I bow, gratefully, to each of you.*

Prologue

My mother, Ria died when I was seven months old. My father, Ronnie died when I was four years old. The first time I died I was nineteen. A series of three death-defying experiences, over the course of my adult life have gifted me, among other things, precious moments of time with my parents. The experiences have also helped me to gain new perspectives on what it means to live, what it means to die, and how this knowledge impacts not only me, but the lives of everyone I encounter. You would think that these experiences would make me live in fear of dying. But instead, because I experienced almost indescribable expansion, true exhalation, and absolute energetic integration all at the same time, there was no fear and no pain. And I don't live in fear of dying today.

Each time, I returned to my waking life with a directive that showed me how to re-set my life's compass towards true north, and bit by bit, the pieces of my purpose started falling into place. I believe that a big part of that purpose is ultimately sharing these experiences with the world. The journey we will take together here will be unimaginable sometimes. From the details of my experiences in the initial chapters, to the lessons I learned in the middle chapters, to my thoughts on what I think it all means towards the end, we are in for quite a ride.

In all of my death and back to life experiences, there were witnesses who can attest to what physically happened to my body. However, my greatest hope, dear reader, is that from my words you will get not only a glimpse, but a real and lasting feeling for how magnificent life is, was, can be, and always will be.

Chapter One
Mother

August 1993, Sarnia, Ontario, Canada

The first time I died I was nineteen and swimming in Lake Huron. It was summertime and I was home with my grandparents on the break between my sophomore and junior year of college. I would be moving in with my boyfriend and two other roommates that fall. That boyfriend decided to come down from Toronto to visit me and meet my family. It was kind of a big deal; we had half-seriously talked about getting married one day.

He was all excited to get into the water, but it was a rough surf day on the lake. The sun was out, but it wasn't all that warm and the waves were coming in fast and high in time with the strong winds. I'm a good swimmer and didn't think it was a smart idea to go out in it, but I'd told him so many stories about swimming out to the sandbar that he was determined to go and teased me about being a chicken.

I'm almost six feet tall, but he stood over six-two and was more confident about striding into the water and ducking under each foaming wave. I kept up as best I could, but I was falling farther and farther behind him. When I couldn't touch the ground anymore, I tried not to panic—that section where you can't touch the bottom anymore is brief, you only have to swim for a little bit before the little miracle of sandbar emerges and you practically stub your toe on it. But I wasn't finding it. The waves were all around me now and I couldn't see my boyfriend's head bobbing ahead of me either. I looked side to side and finally back to shore. I was way over from where we had started; the waves had pushed me almost past the edge of my grandparents' property line. I decided it was too much, something was off, and I resolved to go back to the shore. I treaded water around again to look once more for my boyfriend to try to call to him and tell him what I was doing, but I didn't see him because a wave so big I couldn't see around it was about to crash over my head.

It hit me like an avalanche and for as much time as I've spent in the water and been tossed around, the power of the impact fully pounded through me. It actually felt like it went through my skin and head and exited out behind my heart and entire torso. My body hit the lake floor and I felt the skin of my shoulder scrape against the little rocks, reeds, and debris at the bottom. Stunned and truly frightened I tried to find my feet so that I could push and jump with all my might and make my way back up to the surface. It was so hard to find them, the force of the water still had my feet up above me and I couldn't tell which way was up and which way was down. Finally, I found my feet and I opened my eyes and looked up. I could see the sunlight coming in through the water, but barely; it was so dark and cold down there and I was terrified that I was so far down, and oh yeah, *not breathing*.

Since I couldn't take a breath to push up, I used the muscle strength I had, but it was meagre. I was floating towards the surface, but not fast enough. My arms and legs were flailing and I was wriggling with all my might. I just had to get enough power to go straight up and it seemed like I was still so far away. My ears were ringing and it felt like my chest would explode. It was infuriating and if I could have screamed, I would have. I sensed (hoped) that I was near the surface but I couldn't lift my head to look; I could feel that my legs were coming up from underneath me again. I felt another big wave coming and as my body was pulled down farther still by the undertow, I tried again to get my head up and out of the water but I started to feel detached from the completeness of my body.

Another wave came. This time it smashed me head first right into one of the rusty, metal barriers that line the beaches in that area, ironically to help break the waves and protect property erosion. Everything went black.

I don't know how long I was like that but the next thing I recall was that I could see light again. I was floating in the water but I couldn't hear the waves or anything really, and I could see a far-off light that looked like the sun shining through the water. I thought I must be approaching the surface again and I felt relief. I didn't feel the panic of my lost breath and there was no pain in my body anymore from where I had hit my shoulder or banged my head, just an amoebic like experience of lifting and floating towards the surface. But then, within that circle of light, I started to see things.

People, a building or two, a garden? The people were laughing and happy and the garden was fertile. The sun was shining. Glasses, plates, and cutlery were tinkling. Everyone was having a wonderful time, it seemed. Everyone was wearing white or very light-colored clothing. They looked like movie stars enjoying the views and the Mediterranean weather of Santorini, Greece. I started to recognize some of the people. My aunt Caroline, my great-grandfather Charles, my great-grandmother Flavia. *Wait. Wait. Wait. Wait. Wait. Wait. Wait. Wait a minute. These people are dead.*

A shockwave rose through me as I felt myself lurch forward, being propelled towards it all and I reached with my right hand towards that circle of light, in the direction of these people that I had loved who were waiting there, it seemed, for me. Suddenly, to my right, my mother appeared. I do not remember her in actuality; I was so young when she was killed in a horrendous accident resulting from brake failure and someone else driving under the influence. I grew up in a home filled with her pictures, stories of her beautiful kindness and smile, and a sense that I have never longed for something or someone so much as her. I eagerly floated towards her, relieved to recognize her and be with her at last.

She had on a long baby-blue dress and ribbons were wound in her hair, floating out around her head. She was so beautiful. She had a sound to her that I cannot fully describe, but it was like being in the center of a perfectly-pitched musical note. She reached for me, not to embrace me or welcome me, but to hold me back. Stagnant in the tunnel, I pushed against her. I tried to pull my way through, but she was firm. "It is not your time, Megan," she said. "You have so much to do, children to have, work to do, so much to be. Not yet."

Now I could feel myself dying inside, crushed by her powerful presence and seeming rejection. I couldn't hear or make sense of her message as it felt as if my heart was exploding. I cried out, screamed, yelled, begged, pleaded. I just wanted to be with her. To feel that warmth of her presence. To be in the wave of that singular musical note. One. More. Time. But the answer was not to be what I had hoped. We argued and it was painful. Her voice was firm and feminine and powerful: Not. Yet.

And then I was floating back and away from her and the magnetic pull was reversing and there was nothing I could do about it. I could feel the enveloping warmth of the garden and all of that goodness slipping away. Seconds later, I was zooming through a vortex-like whooshing and roaring experience, and then I was back in Lake Huron, being lifted from the water by my boyfriend.

On the beach, he worked furiously to get the water from my lungs. I saw all this happen from outside, just beside and above my actual body, feeling like a doppelgänger keeping an eye on the other. It was the strangest sensation, like I was spying on myself, and then when the water came out of my lungs I felt myself plummet back into my body. I couldn't make sense of what I was experiencing. My throat was raw, the top of my head was pounding, it hurt to take in air, and I couldn't stop coughing.

The memory of my mother and that place that was so fresh and soft and comforting clashed with the gritty reality of the sand and the cold air and so much bodily pain everywhere. Through all of this my boyfriend was livid. Angry with me. How had I let this happen? Why didn't I stay closer to him? Wasn't I supposed to be such a good swimmer?

I couldn't speak for a while and so I didn't. It hurt to breathe. It hurt to blink. Everything was so bright. It hurt to be back here on Earth and I couldn't focus on anything. I couldn't stop crying or retching. I wanted to talk to my grandparents, who had raised me, and tell them about what I had seen, but I was really scared. Part of me was still lingering in that soft space and that part was resisting and fighting with the parts of me that were back on the windy beach. I was having an incredibly hard time staying in my body and I didn't really want to. I had never felt more confused.

When I could talk and tried to talk about all of this to my boyfriend, he would have none of it; he didn't even want to hear about it. It was all nonsense and I was just irresponsible, not making sense, and being silly. He insisted we not speak of it at all. Ever again. Period. What should have been a moment of warning for me about his temper and controlling behavior did not sink in until the coming winter. There had been other signs, too. Like when we were first dating, he called seventeen times in one afternoon and filled up my roommate's answering machine wondering where I was. But I had thought this was romantic at the time; I was only eighteen and had been flattered. So, I put the incident behind me, told no one, and when that boyfriend asked me to marry him a short while later, I foolishly said yes, thinking that somehow this incident had brought us closer together.

February 1993, Ottawa, Ontario, Canada

My boyfriend and I were back at school, living together in an apartment with our two other roommates. On one of the coldest, snowiest nights I decided to go out dancing with some girlfriends. My boyfriend always disapproved of this activity unless he was invited, so as usual there was tension while I prepared to leave. It began to annoy me that I had a curfew (it's true!), that he expected me to call and check in with him. This was before the time of everyone having cell phones, so checking in was not an easy task. He also wanted me to not talk to certain friends whom he didn't approve of.

I left that night with no intention of following any of the rules. He was starting to feel like an authority figure instead of my boyfriend. I had just turned twenty and needed some freedom, not this. I was regretting my decision to be engaged and told myself since I had no ring anyway, it wasn't really real. While hanging out with my friends that night, we chatted about our lives and I realized I was done. Done with him. Done with pretending that everything was okay. I decided that I was too young to settle for this kind of relationship and it was time to move on. My friends agreed, and one by one they started sharing with me their true feelings about him and me, saying that they were shocked we were still together because he didn't seem to be the right person for me.

One alarming example they recalled was when I had thrown him a surprise birthday party earlier in the year. He had told me, in jest I thought, that he did not want a party. He was very sociable and loved being the center of attention and so I colluded with his classmates to arrange it. Shortly after, we arrived home to the party and everyone jumped out from behind the couches and rooms and all was revealed, he turned to me and "playfully" wrapped his hands around my neck and shook me. It was uncomfortable to say the least and in full view of everyone at the party. While he did not actually squeeze tight enough to choke me, the pressure was enough to know that he was displeased and I would hear more about it later.

That snowy evening I had a blast dancing and being with my friends. I didn't call to check in, I talked to everyone, and I didn't care what time it was. When the club closed, the combination of a city-wide taxi strike and a wicked snowstorm presented a problem getting home. A male friend who had a car and lived a short distance away offered to drive my friends and I home, but we all lived in different places and with the weather disaster it was well after 3:00 a.m. when I got back to the apartment.

He was up, waiting for me with his hands on his hips, absolutely fuming mad. Part of me got it. Maybe he was worried, understandable with the weather. But I knew in that moment, it wasn't that. He just wanted me to do what he said. Period. He pushed me down on the living room couch and with his long index finger in my face, began hissing out his rage. I could feel his saliva spraying my skin. Somehow, I detached myself from my body again and could see from outside myself what was happening. I'd had a fair amount to drink, to be honest, but I sobered up in an instant and just left my body.

He accused me of sleeping around, asking me over and over who I'd been with, who I'd been fucking. I lay there, silent and steady. My own rage was building. He pinned me down flat on the couch. He pressed the top of my chest down with his left palm and began punching the sides of the couch on either side of my head with his right hand. I could feel the air move each time his fist came down. I had my eyes squeezed shut but then I opened them and looked right at him. "Are you going to hit me or not?"

At his size and strength, there was no way I could get out of it so I just wanted to know. He yanked me up to my feet and slapped me hard on the face, towards the left and then the right. Dazed, confused, and stunned I started to fall, but he grabbed me by the shoulders and shook me so hard I could feel my head bobbing around my shoulders. My teeth were clattering together and I got scared. I prepared to run.

I started to wrench away from him and turn to the hallway to run towards our bedroom. If I could get into the bathroom, it had a lock on it. Of course, he caught up with me and grabbed hold of my left wrist with one hand and my throat with the other. I got still. Really still. His hand on my wrist was squeezing so tight it felt like it might break. The hand on my throat was scary too, but not as firm or as strong. I knew he'd need both hands to hurt me more and so I said, in the firmest voice possible, "Let go of me." He smiled and gripped harder. I winced, but said louder, "Let go of me!" When he increased the pressure again, that ringing came back into my ears and I knew this was it. There were three other people in the apartment at the time and they needed to help me. I screamed as loud as I possibly could, "LET GO OF ME!" and it could quite possibly have woken the dead.

Within a moment one of my roommates was in the room telling my boyfriend to release me. He still refused. I kept screaming. Eventually my other roommate's boyfriend, who happened to be staying over that night, came in too, and somehow both of them got him off of me and insisted he get out of the apartment. I sobbed in my room, petrified he would come back.

Within the next few weeks, he moved in with another friend and he slept on the couch the few nights in the meantime. His mother called me, pleading with me to give him another chance, insisting he didn't mean it. His temper just got the better of him, that he was a good person. I was hardened inside to him and there was no room for reconsideration. Absolutely not. NO. My mother was right—I had work to do and he would have no other chances in my life.

Chapter Two
Father

October 2000, Calgary, Alberta, Canada

The second time I died I was twenty-five years old and had just given birth to my second daughter, Jesha. I'd had a rapid labor and delivery. From the onset of intense contractions to transition and pushing, the amount of time it took for her to be born was about an hour and a half. We had a room reserved at the hospital but there was no time to get there. We called our doula, Kimberly, when things got intense, but it was just after 4:30 p.m. and she was coming through rush hour traffic. She advised us to get into the bath and try to relax until she arrived.

When she arrived, close to 6:00 p.m., she could see Jesha's head crowning and told me to start pushing as the urge arose. She could call an ambulance, but was honest in saying that she didn't think they would make it in time either. I was okay with that; I had wanted a home birth all along.

Jesha was born just a few minutes after 6:00 p.m. but the cord was wrapped around her neck and there were some careful adjustments that Kimberley needed to do to unwind the cord and allow her to descend safely. Birth is never an easy process, but I had no idea how much more intense it was about to become.

The sun was setting to the west over the Rocky Mountains of Canmore and Banff, and I looked out my bedroom window at them as she came into the world. We had moved to Calgary about two years earlier for a job promotion I had received, and I was elated to be in a town where my closest cousins lived and to be in such proximity to the mountains. The winters could be brutal and snowy, but in October it's still pretty mild. It had been a lovely fall day and the golden sun setting over the mountain peaks made me feel so incredibly grateful and at peace, living in a place where I could witness such stunning beauty every day.

Shortly after she was born and determined to be in ideal health, it was time to get me into the shower and prepare for the afterbirth arrival. My first daughter, Sandelle, had been born in a hospital and the circumstances had been radically different. And while I doubt that anyone feels particularly physically great after giving birth, I have to say that I felt quite bad in that moment, totally different than after I'd had Sandelle three years earlier. I attributed it to the fact that I'd had no surgical or anesthetic intervention this time. With Sandelle, I'd had an epidural and an episiotomy, so I thought this sinking, breathless feeling I was having was the result of a totally natural childbirth.

My husband, Richard, who I'd met and become friends

with while I was struggling with my boyfriend, was now my rock, my hero, my lover, and my very best friend. It is amazing how the disaster of one situation can wholeheartedly catapult you into the glory of something so beautiful and fulfilling. He had been nervous about giving birth at home and was against the idea, which was why we had reserved the hospital room. He was now working hard with Kimberly and my friend Jeanette, who had also attended many births and was an experienced caregiver, who came over right afterwards, to get me settled into bed right away.

The afterbirth experience in the hospital with our previous daughter was something that was done to me. Anesthetized and spent, I recall my doctor at the time telling me to push as hard as I could while she pulled it out. It was a mild sensation. This time, Jeanette (Jeannette was actually my doctor but it was against the law for her to attend a home birth, however she came afterwards and did this part) was telling me to push (without her pulling) and I couldn't do it. I was freezing, shaking, and bleeding like crazy. I had given birth on the floor of our bedroom on a shower curtain and at the very last moment, my foot slipped and inadvertently kicked the shower curtain out from underneath me as Jesha was coming out. She and everything else in my uterus ended up on our snow-white carpet. I was continuing to bleed profusely, but the carpet was the last thing on my mind.

To help me relax, Jeanette ran the shower for me, helped me to get in and try to warm up. But no matter how hot she set it, I couldn't get warm and continued to bleed, a lot. The bathroom was full of steam and the water was as hot as it could get without scalding me. I couldn't stand; I had to sit in the bath and let the shower wash over me. We tried again to move the afterbirth, but I couldn't push. I couldn't breathe, it felt like my chest was caving in, my head was becoming detached from my body, and my heart was pounding in my ears. I told her something was wrong. I could feel myself getting light-headed, breathless, and panicked. I just wanted to lie down with a big snuggly blanket in that small bathtub that my six-foot frame could barely fit into.

Jeanette held my chin in her hands and tried to lock eyes with me. I couldn't focus but I heard her tell me that it was really important that I push. That it had to come out or I would continue to feel worse, and that it could become a life or death situation. So, she helped me by pulling a bit and somehow, I pushed. When it came out, it was like giving birth all over again and still I bled more. I was scared and so, so cold. I still couldn't stand to move out of the bathroom and back into my bedroom, so my husband and Kimberly—who are both pretty tall—put one of my arms around each of their shoulders and held me up, instructing me to take one step and then another towards the bedroom directly adjacent to the ensuite bathroom. At first, I couldn't feel my feet, then my legs, and when I tried to speak, everything went black.

When I opened my eyes, I was on a stretcher in a hospital hallway, doctors and nurses running everywhere. *Of course*, I thought, *I ended up at the hospital anyway.* But I was sort of relieved because I didn't feel so bad anymore. I looked to my left and suddenly my father was standing there, the man whom I hadn't seen alive since I was four.

July 1978, Toronto, Ontario, Canada

He'd had a massive heart attack at the Toronto airport and when help arrived, he was already gone. Witnesses say that he stumbled, appeared to clutch at his chest and heart area, and then fell to the ground, unresponsive. I didn't live with him after my mother died; my mother's mother, Madeline had taken me in to live temporarily with her and my mother's stepdad, Chester, until my own dad could get himself together.

The trauma of my mother's death had affected him so greatly that he was unable to work. He moved in with his brother and he generally detached himself from the world. Unable to parent and barely able to look after himself, he consented to let them temporarily have custody of me until he could figure things out. Well, he never quite got things in order, but he did come and visit me at my grandparents' house usually twice a year, at Christmas and during summer vacation.

I didn't understand who he was growing up and my first memory of seeing him when he came to visit one Christmas was thinking he looked like the comedian Richard Pryor or JJ from the TV show *Good Times*. I remember my grandmother telling me to "say hello to your father." I didn't understand what she was talking about and I was scared. My father and who I called "Dad" was my grandfather Chester. I don't recall this part, but I am told that I called my biological dad "Uncle Daddy" because I apparently theorized if you visited twice a year you earned the name "Uncle" before the name "Daddy."

Ronnie was tall and skinny, smoked a lot of cigarettes, and had a big round afro and facial hair. When he walked down the street, people stared. Could it be because he was so tall, good-looking, and fashionable? Maybe, but he was also the only black man most people had ever seen around a mostly-white, Catholic town, so I'm sure that had something to do with it too. I can recall us walking to the park or the beach when he visited and getting stares. My mom was white and had been born in Belgium before immigrating to Canada. People are never totally sure what to make of me—but his over six-foot frame, thick moustache, brown skin and afro made him undeniably black and stare-worthy in the late 1970s.

Ronnie did not pay very much attention to me and I don't say that to blame him. I understood even at a very young age that he was a shell of a man. He walked, talked, smoked, ate and drank, but he roamed the halls of the house at night because he couldn't sleep. He never looked me in the eye and certainly did not want to play games or cuddle. Even when we walked down the street together, he did not want to hold my hand. He would tell me I was a big girl and to stay close by him and walk on my own. It frustrated me that he didn't work the way regular parents were supposed to work. On the beach, he would stare at the waves and smoke. If I sat down beside him, he did the same thing. If I rolled around in the sand, did jumping jacks, shouted at the top of my lungs and got dirty, he did the same thing. It felt like I didn't exist in front of him. He was just not there. I can't even remember his voice because he spoke so little.

Calgary, Alberta, Canada, October 2000

So, you can imagine, that when he appeared beside my hospital bed in the year 2000, I was quite stunned. He was dressed like a 1970s sitcom character: brown leather jacket, beige ribbed turtleneck and brown corduroy pants. The afro was a little smaller, but it was him. I tried to reach for him calling out, "Dad!" I was so excited. It didn't occur to me just yet how this was all happening. It felt incredibly real. He actually looked at me, with concern in his eyes. This is the only time I can recall him looking right at me.

I tried to tell him he had another granddaughter and what her name was, but he stopped me mid-sentence and said,

"You're not supposed to be here, Megan. Just stay right here, I'll be right back."

He ran off down the hallway while my rage built up again. Here we were, more than twenty years later and he still wouldn't *talk to me?* It was beyond my comprehension. I couldn't get up anyway (yes, I tried) and in a minute or two he came running back with people dressed in full medical gear. He was panicked and kind of angry. He was gesturing frantically for them to get to me. I just wanted to talk to him and connect with him. I couldn't see the faces of the staff; they were scrubbed up and wearing surgical masks. They began hovering over me and I could feel their hands on me pushing and prodding and I was trying to fight them off so I could talk to my dad, The next thing I knew I was back in my bedroom at home in Calgary.

Hovering above the bed, I saw them working on me, trying to get my body to function again. The actions and what I was seeing and feeling made no sense at all. I could feel the immense tension in the room, even panic. Finally, I opened my eyes to a blow. Richard was slapping me lightly across the face back and forth, back and forth. Kimberly was doing chest compressions. I wasn't quite back in my body yet, and I was watching this rather than feeling it. I could sort of feel the pressure from Kimberly's palms pumping at my chest and feel my chin going side to side. I could see Richard's beautiful brown face had turned a shade of green I didn't think was possible. Kimberly was sweating and panting and kind of yelling as she counted.

When I opened my eyes fully and tried to take a breath I couldn't, and it felt like when I was underwater again at nineteen trying to find air and fight my way to the surface. A final slap from Richard prompted a sharp intake of air that got me breathing again. It was so painful; it felt like I was inhaling and swallowing glass.

Kimberly was shaking and commanded that I needed to get to the hospital right away. I was bleeding heavily and my heart had stopped. I was insistent that I wasn't going anywhere. Now that I was back in my bed and my baby was born, all I wanted was to rest and be still. Kimberly honored my wishes but said if my bleeding did not decrease within ninety minutes of taking homeopathic arnica supplements every fifteen minutes, she would insist on calling an ambulance and have me brought to the hospital regardless of what I wanted. Somehow, in that time period the bleeding slowed and I sank back into my own body once again.

This time was different. I'd had two experiences in which I definitively died—once seeing my mother and the other seeing my father. What did this all mean? Obviously, we all have a purpose here, and now I was a mother twice over and a wife. We had a lovely home, careers, extended family and friends that we adored. What was I supposed to be doing differently? The first experience I attributed to a literal shake up that needed to happen between myself and my then boyfriend. But now? I would have said I was pretty happy, balanced and on the right path, but I guess I was wrong. My father hadn't actually said why it wasn't yet time to go, frustratingly leaving me as usual on my own to figure it out. My mother had told me the reasons why, even if I had disagreed with her in that moment out of emotional angst. But my father hadn't said a whole lot, other than it wasn't right, it wasn't my time yet. So, what now?

Chapter Three
Family

January 2004, Cambridge, Ontario, Canada

The third time I died was the day after I turned twenty-nine and I was driving in a wicked snowstorm to work. We had moved back to southern Ontario for a job opportunity for Richard in 2002. The Cambridge area of Ontario where we had moved is part of a severe snow belt and this day was one for the record books.

With near zero visibility because of the falling snow and cold temperatures that rapidly create patches of black ice on roadways, it was a malicious concoction to drive in. Richard and I both had quite a commute to get to our jobs and our girls were involved in a complicated mix of daycare, babysitting and Sandelle being in kindergarten for half the day. I had started a new job the month before and although my commute was a bit shorter than my previous job, it was still about forty-five minutes on a good day. On this morning the snow was coming down but good.

I was managing a small home and accessories gift store and had to get to work to open the doors and get set for the day. As I travelled down the on-ramp to get to the highway, going less than thirty km per hour, I pressed my foot on the clutch of my four-wheel drive Subaru Forester to gently ease into third gear and prepare to merge into the slow-moving and sparse highway traffic. I felt a momentary lurch in the car and then another lurch in my stomach as I sensed what was about to happen.

The car had hit a patch of ice and as it started to swing to the side, totally out of my control, it was that exact feeling you get when you go on the tilt-a-whirl ride at the county fair. Except, it didn't stop. The car swung one way, then another. I couldn't tell which way I was facing anymore, and as it began to spin in full circles, I prayed that I wouldn't hit anyone because there was nothing I could do. When the car stopped spinning, I looked up and around and all I could see was white. I felt a surge of relief; *I must be on the shoulder, off to the side.*

Just then, the grill of a double tanker truck hauling thousands of gallons of milk rammed right into the passenger side of my car. The sight of that looming grill, probably two or three times taller than my car is something that I've never really been able to shake from my memory. The scale and immensity of what was happening had me realize, absorb, and accept immediately that this was it. I was not going to survive this.

Everything moved in slow motion after that, the sound of crushing metal, bursting glass. Although heavy snowfall makes quiet sounds, there was nothing that could mute the collision of metal on metal. I could hear the roar in my ears and I immediately left my body and zoomed up into the atmosphere. I watched from above and yet could feel my body being thrown about in the car, even with my seatbelt on. It felt like it was happening in a padded room; I didn't feel the pain of the impacts in those moments. It was almost comical.

Meanwhile, the car had flipped over twice and only stopped because it hit a concrete shoulder barrier at the side of the road, without which my car in all likelihood would have continued to roll on down the hill that was right behind it.

My consciousness completely floated up and over the car and I could see through the blizzard snow all around me. I wasn't cold and I felt elated and ecstatic and kind of like I was a piece of snow even as I was looking at the millions of other snowflakes. No sound, just a blanket of softness all around me, a sparkling feeling. A good feeling. Everything is perfect and wonderful and okay feeling. I wasn't confused any more. I didn't feel pain and I wasn't being thrown about. I wondered how I had ever thought snow was cold. It was beautiful and warm, like a soft blanket.

What happened next was a film reel of my life. Every single happy, joyful, glorious, emotion-filled moment of my life swirled around me. My wedding, my children, swimming (believe it or not), dancing, being held by my parents as a baby, feeling the sunshine on my skin, lying down in the grass. Watching Sandelle run to her classroom wearing her purple puffy coat and turning to wave at me and smile one more time. The smell of Jesha all soft and warm and cuddly when I picked her up from her crib. Richard and I laughing. Riding my banana-seat bike with streamers on the handlebars with my friends. Getting ice cream on a Friday night and feeling the tightness of a sunburn on my nose and cheeks from a day spent at play. It was literally all the good memories of my nearly thirty years compressed into a home movie reel that kept playing on a loop where more and more of the joy kept being revealed in new and wonderful ways. I felt light, I felt ready; I was going home. Except, I was not. Of course, I was not.

I started to hear the sound of a man crying and could feel myself being pulled downwards. I surmised that I was now at my funeral and someone, perhaps Richard, was wracked with grief, and I was trying to figure out how to bring comfort and reassurance from beyond that it was going to be okay. I ached for my girls too, and thought about how losing their mother at such a tender age would affect them. I recalled my own mother passing and wondered if it was our fate to keep losing our mothers so young, time after time.

Then, I was cold again. *Wait, wait a minute. If I'm cold I can't be in that space anymore where you don't feel pain, discomfort and separation.* The sobbing grew louder. I got colder. I blinked my eyes open to see that I was still seated in my car. All the windows were smashed in and there was snow and glass everywhere. All over me, all over the inside of the car. My entire right side was numb and my head hurt horribly. Holy shit, it was cold. But who is doing that crying, which I can *still hear*?

I looked out the front of my car to the right and saw a man bent over beside my car, one hand on the crumpled hood, and he was just sobbing and apologizing and praying and saying "OH GOD!" over and over and over again. I tried to move, but I was buckled in and my seat was kind of jammed up towards the door. *I want to help him; he thinks I'm dead and wonder of wonders, I'm actually not.* I could hardly believe it myself. I managed to call out something; I think I just said hello or hey and he stood up slowly to peer into the car at me.

"You're ALIVE?!" he screeched and began again with the "Oh my Gods" and full-throttle panic. He ran back to his truck and then back to my car and explained that he had already called the police and they were on their way. Other people on the highway began to pull over and stepped out to help. They offered blankets, their own coffee or tea they were sipping on, and all sorts of comforts. I will be forever grateful for the grandest and kindest of humanity that was shown to me that day.

More than half an hour passed and due to the weather, numerous other accidents and blockages had since occurred, but still the police had not arrived. I felt okay, not perfect, but okay. I wanted to get out of my car, which had no protection from the snow and wind and cold anymore and get into the car of someone who had stopped and offered to help. It was well below zero and I was going into shock. The woman who had stopped had a cell phone and asked if I wanted to call anyone. I wanted to call my husband, which I did, and I don't remember what I said because I got his work voicemail. He said I just screamed and cried into the phone and he couldn't tell if I was dying or not, and he saved it for six months afterward and listened to it every day as a reminder that I was still alive and had come back to him, again.

The truck driver and the woman who stopped argued over whether or not I should get out of my crumpled car. He thought I should stay put and wait for paramedics, whereas she could see that I was able to move and needed to get out of the cold. We were pushing on forty-five minutes in subzero weather. I crawled out of my driver's side window and limped to her car where she had a warm wooly emergency blanket and hot tea to share. I remember her talking to me but I don't know what she said. I just shook and sipped, and even though she had her heat blasting high, I was still cold.

The fire department arrived first and they asked me why I had gotten out of the car and where my children were. My children? My children? What do you mean my children?

The firefighter said that there was a crushed and twisted car seat in the back; where was the child that would sit in it? And I couldn't remember. It is impossible to explain to you the absolute terror that went through me. I thought my insides might drop out of me right at that moment. He saw the look on my face and all hell broke loose. Every firefighter jumped down from the truck and began combing the roadside, scrambling down the hill behind the shoulder barrier. Digging through the snow. I was trying to stay conscious and closed my eyes and tried to breathe. Then I remembered. I had dropped Sandelle at kindergarten that morning and Jesha at the babysitter's. I ran back out to them and the frantic search for my babies ended while I bawled.

Paramedics showed up and immediately told me I probably had a head injury because I had been unable to recall where my children were; they started taking a closer look at me. They asked me what day of the week it was and when my birthday was. Funny enough, I could remember that my birthday had been the day before and that I had turned twenty-nine, but I couldn't remember the actual date or day of the week. I was adamant that I was not going to the hospital though. It's almost impossible to explain why I so strongly refused to go to the hospital. Richard thinks it's because I thought I might die at the hospital, as my mother did, but my rationale was, *Heck, this was third time I've been through this and was alive, so what would be the point of that?* In my mind, I was not going and that was that.

Besides, I could hear the police scanner reporting accident after accident after accident and was sure I would be okay; not everyone who got into an accident that day would be.

The paramedics disagreed with me, but couldn't force me to go and so they had me sign a waiver and then had the tow truck driver bring me home, which was less than five minutes away from the scene of the accident. Once home I watched the bruising increase and spread up on my leg, arm, ribs—all along the right side of my body. I shook and cried and wondered about Richard, the girls, and work. I just wanted to be warm and safe again. I fell asleep and about two hours later awoke to the sound of a loud motor. We lived in a cul-de-sac at the time and so I limped towards the front door and saw a tow truck with Richard's car sitting on it and Richard *limping* towards me.

What in the actual holy hell? My husband and I made the local news that evening as emergency services realized that as soon as they cleared my accident, my husband, racing home to figure out what happened to me spun out in his car in the *exact same intersection*, hit the highway median, crushed the front of his car and had his dashboard collapse on his legs. He, too, refused medical treatment because he was so anxious to get home to see me. We stood in the front hallway of our home and bawled together.

When we called the insurance company, they started an investigation into a domestic violence incident because they initially thought we had somehow purposefully tried to ram into each other on the highway. After a lot of explaining by him and crying by me, they sent a rental car company representative to pick us up and bring us to get a temporary vehicle until everything was sorted out. We had to go to where our cars had been brought to get pictures to submit for insurance reimbursement.

When I saw my crumpled pop-can looking car, my knees gave out beneath me. Looking at the remains of that car, I had no idea how I survived and the agents who were with us told me the only reason I lived is because of the reinforced frame of Subaru cars. The combination of impact, flipping and force would have probably killed me had I been driving Richard's sedan. Luckily, Richard spun his car but didn't flip it, so his leg was sore and bleeding a little from the dashboard collapse, but he was essentially okay.

We decided to go to the walk-in clinic together after all that. Doctors were originally concerned that both of us might have fractures in our right tibias and I might have a concussion. Miraculously, neither of us had any major injuries or fractures. I continued to bruise up pretty bad over the next week or two and was generally sore, but I was okay.

The result of this combined double accident was that family needed to come first. Our commutes were ridiculous. Richard often travelled for ninety minutes to two hours each way to get to work and my commute was unnecessarily long as well. We sold our home in a more rural area and moved closer to the city where we worked so we could be within thirty minutes of our jobs and be able to spend more time with our kids and each other.

I also came to the rapid realization that the small company I was working for was extremely unethical. Their reaction after my accident was, "Well, when are you coming back to work?" after spending just one day at home. They also began pressuring me to fire several long-term employees, including one who was pregnant and then hire new employees at a cheaper rate. I didn't appreciate their behavior towards me or my coworkers. I returned to that job for about two weeks and gave my notice, and just like that, we were moving. I found a new job I was excited about and we were about to embark on a journey that would finally take me in the direction I was supposed to be going.

Chapter Four
Dreamer

Beginning when I was very little, about age four, I began to have a re-occurring dream that was quite terrifying involving a very violent death. It didn't make sense in my young mind and when I tried to explain it to my grandmother, she would good-naturedly reassure me that a bad dream is just that, a bad dream. But here's the thing. I also had not only vivid and re-occurring dreams, but I then would witness some of the things I dreamed about coming true in waking life. So you can imagine, if I have one scary (or not scary) dream come to fruition— *what about the other ones?*

This particular one I'm about to tell you stuck with me and felt so real. Every dream doesn't have real life significance, but if it keeps coming back, it forces you to look at it or your life in one way or another.

The Dream

It is night and I am walking down a cobblestone street. There are gas streetlights burning, but there's not much light and I can't see more than a few feet in front of or behind me. I'm scared. I think someone is following me, but when I turn around to look, I see shadows, nothing definite. It is damp and doesn't smell very good. I walk faster and can feel and hear my shoes tapping on the cobblestones. I didn't develop the language for this dream until I approached closer to ten years old, but I had been having the same dream, all along, over and over and over.

As I walk faster, I sense that whatever is behind me is also moving in. I think I hear a bit of laughter or a snicker, which makes me feel more afraid. When I look down, I don't recognize myself. I have a long, dark skirt on and a tightly buttoned up blouse. I feel constricted like I have layers of clothing on and probably a corset. My hair is long but it is tied up somehow; I can't see my reflection anywhere but I know this to be true. I'm sweating and trying to get home and I'm going as fast as I can. Why isn't anyone else out on the street to help me? Why can I feel the danger, but not see it?

I turn around again and see just the tip of a black top hat and an eyebrow and eye directly beneath it. A gentleman? But no, there is not enough time because he, it, whatever it is, is upon me. There is roaring in my ears; does it come from his lips or mine? The pain in my middle is excruciating. Through the blouse, through the corset, through my skin and organs it sears and scoops and then the air is thin, and I can feel my body lowering to the ground and being dragged away while the rest of me flies up and floats over and away to a field and skies and stars. There is no more pain except for the memory of the cruelty and the lost chance I did not have to escape it.

When I was about twelve, I saw a preview on television for an upcoming movie of the week about Jack the Ripper. I was frozen to the screen. I watched movies, I read books. I was and always have been a voracious reader but I had somehow never come across the story of Jack the Ripper. I'm not even saying that this is definitively the case, but I do feel that there is a connection. I have no proof, only what I have experienced to back me up.

When I told a university friend one night after having a few drinks about this dream I kept having, she asked me if I'd ever heard of past lives. I had not. Raised in a repressive and religious Catholic family, this was totally unheard of to me. In addition to my vivid dream life I also "saw" things, especially around our very old house that we lived in from when I was age two to age ten and that my grandparents were renovating from the ground up. I could write another book about those experiences alone, but I will say that my adoptive sister Tisha (my grandparent's daughter, my biological Aunt) and I both saw a ghostly family descending the front hallway stairs at our house at the same time once. While I was relieved that someone else could finally see what I saw, she took it very hard. She was a teenager at the time and it affected her very badly. In combination with having seen a scary horror movie recently and then seeing figures moving about in our old home, she was sent to counselling with our parish priest to talk her down from her "imagination."

The past lives thing kind of stayed with me, and so from about age twenty onward I started to read about it a little, watched some programs on the History Channel, and had limited conversations with like-minded souls that I met over the years. I wondered, over time, if my experiences with life and death and the possibility of past lives had anything to do with each other. All the while I lived my life, I raised my girls, I went to work, and eventually I went back to school.

In my mid-thirties I started painting and drawing, making artwork of all kinds for my own pleasure. Many of the things I was creating were a direct result of the dreams I was having or things that I saw that others didn't. I became so involved with the art that I decided to enroll in school full-time and get an art degree. Capturing visions through the camera and working both on film and in digital form became my forte and I went so far as to eventually complete my Master's Degree in photography.

February 2008, Oakville, Ontario, Canada

In my second year of undergraduate work in art at the University of Toronto, I was enrolled in a Design and Digital Media Class. The program I was in required all the offered art mediums be taken at least once, and then in your third year you could narrow in on one or two mediums to use in your graduation thesis. Design had been particularly challenging for me because of the use of digital technology.

Creating something by hand, physically was one thing; creating and altering it on a computer was a subject that I struggled with for a long, long time. I was convinced I would fail the course because I would never get it, and then something interesting happened.

We got an assignment where we had to tell a story in a format that was to be both a physical book and a digital representation. In both versions we had to be able to "turn the page." It's somewhat challenging to explain, but the template in InDesign and Illustrator we were to use involved learning how to place your imagery and text in such a way that it always unfolded as a book and you would be graded according to how successful you were in achieving that. I'll say now that this course and this assignment by my teacher, Jay Wilson, changed my life.

Rather than panic about the assignment, I decided to get really excited about the story. Since I was a child I have loved writing; I had initially wanted to be a writer and enrolled in journalism school only to realize I didn't want to write about politicians and murderers; I liked more positive and truthful endeavors. Here was a chance. I decided to tell the story of my re-occurring dream in a comic book format. It would be exciting and dramatic and if I could focus on the story and the images, maybe I wouldn't be so overwhelmed with my learning curve and the challenge of digital media.

I spent so much time and energy on this project I can

hardly explain it. I became as singularly obsessed and focused on this project as I could possibly be. I wanted it to be as perfect as possible, as close to the experience as I could get it. When the time finally came to present it to the class and the teacher, they were speechless. My heart sank, I had blown it. Then my teacher asked why I had decided to write a story about Jack the Ripper. He knew I was a mom and a wife and kind of suburban, so he was perplexed as to why this particular story had interested me enough to invest so much time and energy into talking about it. Up until this point I had not explained to the class that it was actually based upon a re-occurring dream and that a friend had one time casually suggested it might have something to do with past life theory. So I said all that. To the class of thirty-three students and my teacher. Again, everyone was pretty silent.

The following week was our last class of the year and involved the handing out of final grades. Not only did I receive the highest mark on that assignment, but I also received the award for most improved student. I finished with an overall A in a class I thought I might not even pass. But that's not even the best part. Since I presented that project, *I have stopped having that awful dream.* Not one more time has it come back. After thirty years of carrying around that weight, it's just gone.

Chapter Five
Asana

August 1985, Sarnia, Ontario, Canada

When I was about eleven and had hit one of the roughest patches of waking life so far, I accidentally found yoga. Pimply, tall, and with seriously frizzy afro hair and braces, I was the epitome of pre-teen angst, insecurity, and misery. I was struggling in math and science at school and was the proverbial only kid of color in a class full of white Catholic kids. I had friends, don't get me wrong, but I was not excited about my life or my prospects to say the least. I spent a lot of time with books, television, and candy to soothe my psyche.

One weekend, while going to garage sales with my grandparents who loved to look for antiques this way, I came across a deck of cards. For the twenty-five cents or whatever it was, I thought I would amuse myself with a game of Solitaire or Go Fish with my younger cousins that I often baby sat. When I got them home, I was surprised to see that it was actually a deck of cards about yoga poses. A perky blond lady was pictured on each card doing all kinds of—what looked like to me—stretching.

I sorted through them, picked the ones that I thought looked doable and started doing it while watching TV.

There was no mention that I can recall of vinyasa, ashtanga, hatha or any of the commonly used eastern philosophical yoga styles we hear about today. I don't even think there were any words at all on the cards, just the Christie Brinkley wannabe doing all sorts of weird looking things. Somewhere in the deck it must have said to breathe deeply because I remember doing that and it got easier to get into and hold the pose. After that summer though, I probably only returned to the cards once again in winter, but I do recall that when I did it, I felt better, I slept better and my dreams were more peaceful.

January 1999, Calgary, Alberta, Canada

I was pregnant with my second daughter, Jesha and ecstatic to be pregnant again. Our daughter, Sandelle had been born two years earlier and was the little lovey of our lives. Full of personality and energy, she longed for a sibling to play with and Richard and I felt it was a good time to try again. We were in a position to buy a home in the next year or so and it had taken a year of trying before we got pregnant with Sandelle, even though we had both still been in our twenties at the time. We were concerned it might take time again to conceive and so on New Year's Eve 1999 we decided to toast to making another baby and started trying.

We were hoping it would coincide with a 2001 new parental leave guideline in Canada where you would have one-year paid maternity leave, a huge update to the current six-month paid leave. I was in love with the idea of being able to be home for a full year with my children and not have a major loss of income threaten the ability to grow our family.

Two weeks later, we were pregnant. Ha! Jesha was now due to be born sometime in October, a good two months shy of the new parental leave. We embraced our good fortune to have conceived so early and tried not to lament that I would only have six months to be home with them. Conscious that many countries do not even have any sort of maternal paid leave programs in place, we surged ahead with buying a home that we could hopefully close on before the new baby arrived.

I was stressed though, with a toddler and a baby on the way and a busy full-time job, and my doctor wanted to make sure that I got the care that I needed to have a smooth pregnancy and delivery. (We already know how that turned out!) It was because of this that yoga came back into my life.

My doctor referred me to a pre-natal yoga group that met at a church a few blocks away from my house once a week. She said it was important for me to get there, get back into my body, and breathe and move for my baby and for me. My neighbors thought I was weird, but I kept going and didn't care. It did feel good; we were new in town and it gave me a chance to meet some other women besides people I worked with and managed.

I was running the entire western branch of a major home furniture, accessories and design store at that time and had a lot of responsibilities. A lot of people worked "for" me and upper management frowned upon and even warned me formally about being friends with people who reported to me.

The pre-natal yoga teacher was the hairiest woman I had ever met! She was short and muscular and literally vibrated with power. She was astounded to see me as from my voice on the phone she was convinced I would be blonde and petite and look like a cheerleader. So much "HA." Regardless, she was a gift and brought into our classes a dose of spirituality, and an awareness of breath and body that I'd never experienced before.

For our final pre-natal yoga session she brought in Aboriginal drummers who formed a circle and pounded their drums in rhythmic ways while we rested in savasana. I cried and experienced what I now know were deep meditative visions of guardians, wise women, and other things which I cannot name. I found myself quite overcome with the experience and didn't know what to do with it. The teacher advised me to accept the gift of this awareness to myself, my baby and my family and she invited me to continue the yoga with her after the baby was born, but I have to admit that at that time I was not ready for the combined experiences of power, visioning, and confidence that yoga had presented to me.

November 2007, Oakville, Ontario, Canada

After returning to art school, I had a scare with my reproductive health. Pain and heavy bleeding revealed cysts on my right ovary. There was a two-week period of investigation where we didn't know if it was cancer or not and honestly, I was okay with it. It was almost a joke now. I had died three times already; was death really waiting for me this time? I wasn't truly fearless though. Richard was concerned and I had two little girls about to embark on pre-teen years.

When the cysts turned out to be benign, I had laparoscopic surgery to remove them as they were still causing me great pain and heavy bleeding. While in surgery my obstetrician noted that I also had endometriosis. This is when the uterine tissue grows elsewhere in the body, besides the uterus. It can and usually does cause pain, heavy bleeding, and difficulty conceiving. We had our two girls and didn't plan on more, so that didn't concern me so much, but I wanted to be without pain and who loves a gushing period?

I started looking at my overall health and lifestyle. While I was technically fine being in the top end of the tier for a healthy BMI for my height, I could realistically lose up to thirty pounds and still be healthy. Could a lower weight and healthier lifestyle help with endometriosis? Some studies suggested this was so.

I began running and watching what I ate. I dropped ten pounds within a couple of months and felt great. I ran more. Then my knee went. No running. GREAT. Now what? My doctor suggested yoga; she was encouraged by my zest for movement but I couldn't do anything high impact until my knee healed. While in a department store one day I found a DVD that supposedly connected yoga and dance. I had always wanted to take dance lessons and yoga seemed to keep popping up in my life, so this sounded good to try in the privacy of my own home.

This was another one of those moments where there was a big shift. I sweated so hard those first few home yoga sessions, I couldn't figure out what the heck was going on. This was nothing like the pre-natal yoga I had done and nothing like the card game yoga either. I was pumped. I was excited. I couldn't wait to get home each night to do my yoga DVD. I did this for a year and a half at home and gradually worked running back in too, alternating vinyasa and hatha style yoga and running. Eventually, I bought a couple more DVDs with Pilates and other types of yoga; I was hooked! When I practiced and did the closing meditation, I saw and felt things that made me think I could accomplish anything. My dreams were powerful, my artwork was taking off, I felt great and I looked great. I got a modelling contract and appeared in a few catalogs and ads for women's clothing and fashion, at thirty-five!

I told one of my CrossFit friends about my new love of yoga and she said I had to come to one of her favorite classes in a heated studio for power yoga. I immediately said no. To me this was something so private and powerful, there was no way I was going to challenge myself in a way that would have me comparing myself to other people, to risk looking foolish or to try something new and end up falling on my face! As usual, I was wrong about all of that.

Sonja took me to her favorite Sunday night class and yes, it was hot. But I run cold anyway, so I didn't mind the heat. Let me tell you the BAM effect that this class had on me. I could do it. It was fucking hard, but I could holy fucking cow do it! I sweated more than I ever have in my life, but I did it. Savasana was like heaven. The music was perfect. The teacher was like a kindly coach who pumped you up when you needed it and advised you to lie down if you were looking woozy. Sonja and I high-fived each other at the end of class and I barely slept that night. Power yoga junkie, here we come!

Three years later I was still doing hot yoga, but at different studios around town and thoroughly enjoying our community, the feeling of wellness in my body and mind, and opening up more and more to the visions, meditations, dreams and auras that I began witnessing more often. The teachers that I love and the owners of the studio I mainly practice at started asking me when I was going to do teacher training. *I just love yoga, I couldn't possibly teach it, are you crazy?* Once again, I was wrong in my assumption.

The moment happened when I was in a particularly powerful class led by one of the studio owners, Maureen. Yoga by its very nature always involves some sort of self-inquiry, and this class was no exception. With sudden, overwhelming clarity I knew, I absolutely knew, that I had to do yoga teacher training. I had to be able to give back this gift that I'd been given, to someone else. Maybe lots of someone else's. There was no question, no doubt any more that I had something to offer. But how? I was working at a health and wellness center, I was just finishing up my Master's in art, I had student loans, a mortgage, two kids, AAARGH. How was this even sane on any level?

I dissolved into tears on my yoga mat. Luckily, the room is hot and people are sweaty and we were face-down. After class, I couldn't stop my tears and I approached the studio owner about different options to pay for training. I'd been going there so long they offered me an amazing monthly payment plan that was a smaller amount per month over a longer period of time. Still manageable, still doable, still for me. I went home and Richard knew immediately. He sighed and went along with it. And so began my six-month teacher training program that again changed the course of my life.

When I graduated from teacher training, I still had to do thirty hours of volunteer classes. I was scared, but these classes helped convince me I'd done the right thing and that I had something valuable to give back. I taught a few private classes, worked in some corporate fitness centers, and subbed at the studio I trained at. I graduated in May of 2012 from the San Francisco Art Institute with my Master's Degree in Art and Photography and in June of 2013 with my two-hundred-hour yoga teaching certification from IGita in Oakville, Ontario.

In June of 2012, after I graduated, Richard asked me, "What do you want to do now with your Master's Degree?" I wanted to teach and I wanted to practice and suddenly I wanted to move to California. Living in San Francisco part-time while I completed graduate school had shifted my perspective quite a bit on where I wanted to live and what I wanted to do. We decided we would make a plan to move to California, starting first with checking on a long-standing application for a green card that we had initiated over ten years earlier. We got updates about every six months and it never seemed to be going anywhere. We had built our lives in Canada and to be honest, had kind of forgotten about it until now.

Funny how that works, isn't it? A month after we had returned from my graduation ceremony in San Francisco and talked about trying to move there, we got a call—our green card interview was in two weeks. We started looking for jobs and got our house ready to put on the market. After living there for thirteen years that was no small task, but we were motivated.

The first job I applied for I got a call back about it the next day. I had applied for an administrative position at a school, but they were looking for an art teacher! I could not believe my luck. It was summer, classes started in September, how soon could I be there? My head was spinning. I contacted friends in California for help with recommendations of where to live and how to get started; it was all happening so quickly.

My friend and fellow SFAI alumnae, Shirley, helped me find a house to rent, right on her street in a great, safe, family-friendly neighborhood. I gave notice at my job, bought my plane ticket, got my documents in order, and flew to California in October of 2013. I started my art teaching job the week after I arrived and the week after that I also landed a job teaching yoga at the local fitness center. I had two art shows happening and a publication of my work in a major arts journal. It seemed as if all the cards were finally falling into place.

Chapter Six
California

October 2013, Sacramento, California

When I arrived in California, it was like a dream come true for a time. I was fortunate to have landed an art teaching job so quickly, even though it was only part-time. My yoga teaching job, too, was very part-time, just one class per week. But I looked at this time as a valuable opportunity to work on my art, work on my writing, and spend time with my now teenage daughters as they navigated a new school, a new city, and a new home.

Teaching art two days a week sounds pretty awesome, and in many ways, it was. However, the huge challenge of this position was the circumstances of many of the children I taught. Not all but many of the students lived in poverty, in foster care or with more distant relatives, and I came to find out some were actually homeless and spent their evenings sleeping on city buses until they were kicked off. I could not assign homework because most children did not have school supplies at home and often shared rooms with multiple siblings and family members, making realistic completion of homework impossible.

In the six-month period that I taught there, I like to think that I made some sort of difference. There were kids with some real talent and skill and we had an end of year talent show where all of them had the chance to display their artwork, sing or express their creativity in myriad ways. I found myself in tears on many occasions as I witnessed their incredible gifts, drive, and possibilities.

Sadly, a few students were expelled or suspended during that time due to fighting amongst each other or even, on one occasion, attacking a teacher. The school is located in a historically black and impoverished neighborhood and while the high school was making waves of change for university and college acceptance rates and students were really making their way in the world, the middle school adjacent to it where I taught was still struggling to make their mark.

I started in the fall of 2013 part-time with the promise that my position would turn full-time in January of 2014. The funding for this, however, was not approved and my schedule stayed the same. I was teaching more yoga classes by this time, but my employment situation overall needed to change. If I'm really honest I also have to say that teaching kids in this age group was too big of a job for me. I have many friends who are teachers and this job takes a special sort of dedication and level of engagement. I did not have interest initially in teaching anyone other than college or university students. Younger than that age is such a fragile time, and for the kids I was teaching, they had even more to carry in their emotional backpacks than the average kid and it was really tough to handle. While I was never physically attacked, kids certainly can say and do cruel things that are out of line and I was adult enough to know not to respond in kind.

Often, when the kids were especially unruly, we would start class with a meditation. Sometimes it worked perfectly and all thirty-plus students would sit, close their eyes, put their hands together and breathe deeply. At other times, five or six kids would continue to ignore me and talk, but most of the rest of the class would do it. The level of pain, anger and ongoing trauma that they were dealing with was palpable. As a teacher with a black heritage, I know the school was happy to have me there as an example to the kids. They told me so. As the only teacher of color on staff, I spoke about my children often. One of my girls was the same age and grade that most of them were. Being able to show them that someone who looked like them could grow up and teach and become a self-sustaining adult wasn't a small thing. I was aware of this each and every time I came onto campus. The full-time teachers and principal who were there when I was, were and still are doing an amazing job and I wish every single one of them the very best.

When I left, they completely understood that I needed full-time work and I made a special point of telling the kids that they hadn't driven me away. Previous art teachers apparently had told them that their behavior was the cause of a teaching departure and it broke their already wounded hearts. During my time there, I was excited to introduce work to them by nationally and internationally renowned black artists who most of them had never heard of. We did art assignments like silhouettes based on the work of Kara Walker and abstract painting and collage after Jean Michel Basquiat.

I eventually found full-time work with a small company where I stayed for just over three years managing online accounts for art and lighting. I left there, too, after it was bought by a private equity company and everything changed. I had been unhappy for a while and the purchase of the company reinforced the decision I knew I needed to make. I was teaching a lot of yoga. In fact, almost daily and on weekends, too. My impossible dream then was to teach yoga and write full-time, but how?

Chapter Seven
Shakti

March 2016, Sacramento, California

I witnessed the moment of my conception in my friend Sandra's yoga class but it took me weeks to gather the courage to iterate that out loud to her. I realize a statement like that seems so unreal. It took me a few days myself to be able to come to terms with what I knew to be true, but when I hold things back, my life is held back. I had been attending Sandra's classes for a few months and found that yoga was now bringing me a profound sense of self in a very spiritual way. In Sandra's classes, though, it wasn't just the physical practice; in the end, in savasana, I found myself going on pretty amazing journeys. So much so that Richard would say I came home looking and sounding like a different person.

In this particular class, Sandra did a guided meditation into savasana, moving through the different areas of the body from the feet all the way up into the head. I never got past the mid-section of the body. This particular time I travelled to a place I did not totally recognize and yet, it did feel familiar. Tunnels surrounded me that were red and full of dark twists and turns. I was not really scared, just a bit confused about where all this was going.

At this point in my life I knew that I had experienced something called astral projection, several times. Astral projection is considered to be a paranormal phenomenon that involves an out-of-body experience that happens consciously or unconsciously to a person; their consciousness, spirit, essence or soul travels to another space, place or time period. It is similar to death or near-death experiences in that the person can often see their body as if it is someone else and they travel up and out of the body to another place.

These events can be proven in waking life when the person who is projecting comes back with information, facts, and occurrences that they couldn't possibly have actually witnessed in-person. Even as a child, I had experienced this. I've freaked out a few relatives and close friends when I recalled "dreams" where I saw things that they did or happened to them that I had no conceivable way of knowing. I have since met people who purposefully put themselves into this state, and I will admit, I do not know how they do it. Since all of my experiences have been accidental, I am not sure how this works, but I know it's real.

Back in Sandra's class, in these red tunnels, I could tell that this was something internal; this was not astral projection and this was new to me. When I came to a cavern where something was waiting to happen, I could sense it and I waited. An explosion of sorts occurred and I covered my eyes and huddled away. When I opened my eyes, I could see the formation of a tiny little fetus, and in an instant, I knew that it was me. There was a shock of recognition and a dropping kind of feeling in my heart. *Why was I seeing this and what could it mean?*

I wasn't there very long because back in the room Sandra was calling us out of the resting pose and my consciousness was being pulled back into this reality. The next time I saw Sandra we passed each other in the street and she invited me to hear her band play, and Richard, my husband and I went. We became friends and she invited me to a gratitude circle for women. Delighted, I agreed to attend.

When I arrived at the small office on the first floor of a Victorian home for the gratitude circle, I was instantly enchanted. The artwork on the walls spoke to me, the feel of the place was safe and cozy and magical. There were crystals and cards throughout that we were invited to play with, hold or investigate. The kettle was on, ready for tea. The other women there were lovely, full of easy smiles and welcoming arms. It felt good to be there. That day, the circle introduced me to the world of Shakti Rising—a global change organization dedicated to improving the lives of women and girls the world over. But that circle, *that circle*, introduced me to the pathway home that I needed to find for myself.

As we sat through a guided meditation and gentle questions and inter-connection, I became more and more emotional.

I felt like I had finally taken my true seat. Here I was surrounded by these most beautiful, talented, genuine women who had many of the same abilities and gifts that I did. The power of that was overwhelming and I cried softly for most of the time, mortified that I wouldn't be invited back because I couldn't seem to get a handle on my emotions.

That day and in the weeks afterwards, my dreams intensified; I was emotional, but with joy. In July, I attended a weekend workshop with Shakti, dedicated to discovering more about one's own intuitive powers and an introduction to leadership training. I wasn't sure I was ready for it, but I jumped in and I wasn't sorry. I met some of my now closest friends at this experience and as intense as it was, I was ready for more.

In August of that same year I was invited to the Shakti Rising once a year meeting, where everyone in the organization meets to plan the upcoming calendar year. With branches in Hawaii, Oregon, New Mexico, Appalachia, and California, there were potentially hundreds more of these like-minded women. Taking place in Santa Cruz, I drove from Sacramento into the hills and after a few twists and turns when my cell phone signal gave out, I finally made it to the campsite.

There is much about that weekend that I cannot reveal here, that information is and was intended for the women who were there who also experienced it. But I will say this: I broke open on multiple levels and will never be the same because of it. First of all, I had never camped before. Okay, yes, in a camper. Once. But that's it. Here we were, out in the Santa Cruz woods in tents and sleeping bags. I am terrified of bugs; I am terrified of the wild, non-urban outdoors. The first night I don't think I slept because I was so afraid, but after that it was incredible.

I was also working on the Seva team at this event; Seva translates from Sanskrit to English as "Service." So, I was working on a team with other women to help prepare and serve meals for the rest of the women attending throughout the day. I love preparing food, so it was nice to be part of this team and figure out how to make creative and nourishing food with the mostly donated supplies.

One evening that weekend, a group of us were invited to sleep outside in a circle at the top of a hill. How I managed to even volunteer to do that I don't know, but when they asked for volunteers, for whoever felt the most strongly they needed to be there, it seemed like an otherworldly force was moving my legs to step out into the group and say that I, too, was going.

I have to say that the terror as we climbed that trail was real. Everything that I've ever been scared of, real or imagined was coming after me that night. I couldn't see my own hand in front of my face, it was so dark. The thick forest was so silent, it was deafening. The sound of my own breath felt like screeching in the dark. My heartbeat was pounding in my ears.

When we lay down in a circle, our heads all towards the center, we held hands and comforted each other. Me mostly—I was the only one who had never camped out of doors and the other ladies were so kind to reassure me that all would be fine. I was convinced I would be eaten by wild animals, murdered or stolen away and never seen or heard from again.

My dreams and visions that night were legion. It was almost like they were waiting for me to get there, to that spot, so that they could finally come through. To put it jokingly, all the ghosts of past, present and future showed up and had something to say. Not just to me, but to the group as a whole. The next morning, we debriefed with each other and it felt like when we came down the hill, we were each different people.

When I returned from that trip I had a heart-to-heart with Richard. I couldn't go on a trip like that and see the things I did and continue to live day-to-day like all la-di-da. I was profoundly affected and it was at this time that I decided to start finding a way out of my current full-time position with the lighting company. I wasn't being fulfilled by the work I was doing. It would take me another seven months to finally make my exit, but I got the groundwork underway.

I continued to attend gratitude circles and other smaller workshops with the group throughout 2016, and then in May 2017 I was finally was able to go to on a four-day intensive retreat that is intended to start the process of becoming a teacher with them. I was over the moon. By that time I had given notice at my job, received a new job offer at another company, and was ready to go.

Again, what I can logically share here is somewhat limited because Shakti experiences are experiential in their very nature and are reduced and over-simplified by words which can do them no justice. But. I will share what I can.

Yoga, again, transformed this experience for me in a way that I didn't think was possible. Each morning, we started the day with yoga movement, often set to the rising or just risen sun and as grumpy and tired as we might all feel, we always felt great afterwards, ready for breakfast and to start the day's events. However, on the third morning, something was different. These relatively simple movements that I had done hundreds, if not thousands of times before took on another dimension of experience. I found my emotions to be bubbling up, my heart racing, I started questioning everything I had ever believed about myself. Everything.

As we went through the movements, I couldn't see through my tears and eventually I was sobbing and I couldn't stop. When we finished, I was still crying and I asked the teacher, Breyne what was happening. She looked at me kindly and encouraged me to sit and cry and journal, and when I calmed down enough to take in food and drink and again, sit with it and see what came up for me. I realized after following her advice that I was sitting with a new truth. A new truth about myself. About the lies I had told myself my whole life just to be able to get by. To keep smiling. To just keep on keeping on. And it was killing something off inside of me, something that had been my lifeline for, well, my entire life.

I had kept my paranormal experiences to myself or only told those very, very close to me for fear of judgement, retribution, fear of being called crazy, fear of all of that and more. In this society you go to school, you get a degree or three, you get a job, and you keep that job unless you can get a better job because all of that makes sense. *Except, it doesn't make sense if that's not who you are.* I have no regrets about school; I could stay in school for the rest of my life! But what I did regret was that at forty-three years old I was still keeping the most important parts of me a secret, from myself and the world. I was unbearably sad that I had these gifts that had been relegated to the occasional wine-induced conversation with a trusted friend or family member and not shared as the ancestral, life-guiding, and valuable and healing knowledge that it was and could be.

My meditations within Shakti had become so incredible that I had begun to receive messages and images from those gone before, from different times and different places. I was valued and encouraged by my Shakti mentors to keep up this flow of information and to learn to discern what was meant for me personally, and what, if anything, might be meant for anyone else. I hesitate to call myself an oracle and yet, this is what the women closest to me within the group sometimes call me. I don't have a website or a 1-800 number and I'm not selling anything with it. And I'm not passing judgment on those who do—if they truly have the ability to do what they say and offer a service to those who wish to pay for it, I applaud them and am happy for those who receive true insight and guidance. It doesn't work for me in the ways you see on TV, where someone sits before you and asks when the love of their life is going to show up or when they will get pregnant. It's not like that at all for me.

As it happens, I will see someone, sometimes, and oftentimes it's someone I *don't even know* and I will get a flash of information about their life. A lot of times, most of the time actually, it is not pleasant. I have seen that someone is molesting their grandchild; I have seen that someone is going to die an early death; I have seen that someone is cheating on their spouse; I have seen that someone has killed or seriously harmed another person. A lot of the time I just see and feel the suffering and then the reason behind the suffering comes up.

Ironically, for people I am close to, I usually can't see these things and so I often wonder what the purpose of me seeing these random things is at all. What am I supposed to do with this information besides traumatize myself with what I see?

For many years, in my thirties mostly, I purposely shut down my gifts. I hated going to sleep and dreaming about horrific world events that I sometimes woke up to being true the next day. I didn't want these flashes of "insight" into people I didn't know and that didn't seem to hold any good. But working within Shakti made me see things differently again, and once more I had hope that something could be done with this ability. Through Shakti, I met my friend Angie and she introduced me to the next person who would encourage the next big shift in my life.

Chapter Eight
Aureya

Meeting Aureya was like all of my life coming to a full tire-squealing halt in front of me and saying, "Hey, this is exactly where you need to be, so pay attention!" My friend Angie told me about Aureya and explained that she was hosting a psychic school. *I beg your pardon?*

Yes, a psychic school. I was intrigued. This six-month long course was for people who knew they had certain abilities but weren't quite sure what to do with them, or how to harness and focus them. It's funny how things come up on your path over and over again isn't it? How is it that this course seemed to be tailor-made, just for me? Well, it seemed to be tailor-made for about ten of us actually and we all began together in January 2017.

Aureya used to work as a traditional talk therapist and after many years switched her practice to the energetic and healing modalities that she does full-time now. After years of showing and teaching people one-on-one how to work with this energy, she got the idea to start her own coursework and school and enrolled all ten of us, her first students, by word-of-mouth only. As of this writing, Aureya is now in the middle of her third group of ten students and needless to say it's going swimmingly well.

Of the roster of gifts Aureya has to offer, the biggest one she offered me was the ability to be seen. I have mentioned my fears in talking about my experiences, and I told everyone around me who asked, that I was taking a six-month "meditation" course. It wasn't exactly a lie; we did begin every teaching session with a guided meditation and we did spend a lot of time with our eyes closed reading into personal energies. But there again, my truths and myself were being hidden from the world.

Aureya worked with me to help me get more comfortable in talking about what I can see and do, and in July 2017 she invited us all to help her at her booth at a psychic fair in a local park. She would be doing free readings with people and any one of us could also do so. I was not comfortable with doing that and agreed to mind the table and talk to anyone who stopped by and had questions.

At the close of the day, Aureya wanted to take some pictures with those of us who were still there. When she and I went to pose together, I looked her in the eye and smiled, and for a moment, my mother, Ria, was there. She literally popped her head out of her head and smiled at me and there was a sound with it, kind of like a tinkling bell and a soft sighing at the same time. She told me she loved me. I was instantly in tears of gratitude and knew I had made the right decision to take this course and meet this amazing woman and the rest of the women who were there on the journey with me.

During this course, we delved into quite a bit about past lives. I was so thrilled to get into this subject matter, and in fact, Aureya taught us that for many people, it is past-life karma that holds them back in this life *more than anything else*.

Within our first few group sessions we learned to scan our own energy bodies and figure out where our blockages were. I found out quickly that my strongest blockage was in my throat. Surprise, surprise, the Megan truth serum strikes again! For the throat, I learned that sound is a profound energy releaser; for example, singing, humming or even using tuning forks and certain types of vibrations can all help with this. When it came time to work in partners, I teamed up with someone I hadn't known prior to this course.

She immediately saw a past life in me where I had been enslaved; literally I was in chains around my throat and at my hands. I had been truly powerless and subjected to a totally brutal lifetime at the hands of an exceptionally cruel man. I could feel the truth in what she said and saw. She was shaking and on the verge of tears. I could barely swallow as she spoke.

Another woman in the class, Sethyne, who worked with

me later, saw another lifetime where I was not allowed to speak. I had been a scribe who had spent a lifetime writing down the words of others but was not permitted to speak myself.

Another new friend in the class, Elena, saw me in a lifetime as a servant in a household where I had also been forced into unwanted sexual situations at the mercy of the head of the household who did not allow me to speak without permission.

I was in awe of these people who did not know me and yet, saw such detailed and truly convincing past lives that explained a lot about the weight I was carrying with me today. In college, I had innumerable infections of strep throat and throughout my life have had recurrent bouts of "losing my voice." One doctor asked me at one point, "What are you not saying?" At the time she said that to me, I wasn't ready to take a closer look at myself or my life and so the message fell on deaf ears.

Coming into Aureya's group, I felt at home with my abilities and with my group and finally, I too was able to see things about both their lives and mine, past and present, that I was able to share with them and they with me.

One day, overwhelmed by my full-time work, the course material and life in general I checked in with my human resources manager and asked to take a couple of my vacation days. I needed to get away from my day-to-day and do some soul-searching. My neck and back were acting up and I was in serious pain. I was having a hard time extending my right arm as it would tense and spasm almost right up into my ear.

I decided to go to the newly opened Asha Urban Baths, a combination yoga studio and bath house that had a whirlpool tub, steam room, sauna, and cold plunge pool. I just wanted to be in the water and let go. When I got there, I noticed they had massage therapy available. I had only ever had two massages in my lifetime and they had left me in more pain than I came in with and slightly nauseous. But something was telling me that I needed to do this, so even though I hesitated, I asked.

Sure enough, within about half an hour a therapist would be available and in the meantime, I could enjoy the baths. So, I did just that. I soaked and steamed and breathed and tried to let go of all that I didn't need in that moment. When it was time for the massage I let her know what was ailing me and what my past experiences with massage had been like. I can hardly tell you what a miraculous experience this massage was and for several reasons. First of all, an expert, kind and caring touch. She always checked in with me on pressure and pain and gave me advice on how to keep the mobility going when I left. She chided me for being a yoga teacher and yet having so much work to do to relax in my own body.

At one point, though, I kind of drifted away. I was on my stomach with my head comfortably resting in a donut hole kind of pillow so that I could still breathe normally, and then I went somewhere else. Not asleep, because I could still feel her hands and the soft music in the room, but somewhere else.

I was walking up a craggy rock kind of hill and my feet were bare and scratched and dirty. I was sore and tired. I had some kind of a minimal robe or cape on that used to be a beautiful blue, but nothing else. I knew I was naked underneath the thin material. I was so full of sadness that I could feel the weight sinking into my feet with each step. The heaviness in my heart was unbearable. I could feel the tears streaming down my face and my hair whipping about my head in the wind. The sun was setting quickly and somehow it was important that I get to the top before the sun sank below the horizon. The sky was almost totally orange.

This woman who I was seeing and somehow being, someone who I once was, was mourning the death of her young son and her husband. It was a very, very, very long time ago. Her husband had gone off to fight, and in his absence, a local man in power had taken to forcing her into his bed. She had spoken out against him and in punishment he told her that her husband would not come home from the fighting and he made sure it happened. Devastated, she still tried to reject him and he retaliated once more by killing her young son. Thinking she would finally submit willingly with nothing left to tie her to her former life, the man was mistaken.

She climbed to the top of the tallest peak she could find and threw herself off of it to her death where she could join her husband and son forever. That day I met her there and we merged. In the air, as she jumped, I jumped, too. My body met with hers, and this time, instead of plummeting to the rocks below, we forgave each other and she floated up, up, up into the sky, smiling to meet her end rather than falling below on the gruesomeness of the jagged rocks that her body had met before.

Next, I recalled yet another life. I was sitting down and wearing a red robe and brushing my hair, and it was long and black and straight. Funny, since my hair in this lifetime is so curly. This contradiction caused me to stop brushing and look up. There was a mirror there and I was clearly Japanese. It was almost a stereotype of a person that I was looking at, with crimson lips, pale milky face, shiny hair, and beautiful, silky and draped clothing. I knew instantly that I must be wealthy or at least the recipient of very nice things.

Suddenly, a little face appeared in the doorway, pulling the curtain to the side. My son, a little boy about five or six years old, shy and smiling. I reached out to him and he came to me and smooshed himself into my belly and silk robing. I whispered to him in another language that I don't know now, but I was reassuring him and rocking him and he nodded. I can still feel his little head moving. (Both times that I was pregnant with my this-lifetime daughters, I thought I was having sons and was so surprised when they were girls; now I know why!)

When my son left the room and I continued to brush my hair and look in the mirror, my eyes welled up with the painful secret of my son. I could not acknowledge him publicly, for it would be a scandal for someone in my station and for my patron. I was some sort of mistress or kept woman I suppose and in exchange for keeping him quiet, I could keep us both living well. So again, another lifetime of secrecy and keeping my mouth shut.

From slavery to servitude to sexual favor or even downright rape, it was lifetime upon lifetime of never being allowed to be in my own body and mind for my own self. Other lifetimes also came forward and in every one I had been horridly killed—drowning, burning, beating, stabbing, it was unending and immensely sad. In one case, I know that I was only a child when it happened and it was because my mother was the one being punished for her mouth and her abilities and as her child, I was made to suffer, too. So, I could choose to dwell in these memories and lifetimes or I could…? As Aureya put it, it was literally time to let this shit go.

From this lifetime to the many lifetimes ago: relive, forgive, acknowledge, and let go. In freeing this past version of self, I came a step closer to freeing the current version of myself. As painful as it was to recognize, it was true. With each step I took towards that letting go, the more my physical pain retreated. Each step I took, the more my emotional pain retreated. Each step I took, the closer I came towards my true self, my true name, Sat Nam.

Chapter Nine
Sat Nam

Sat Nam is a seed mantra from the Sikh tradition that is often translated as "true name," but it can also be translated as "truth is my identity." Pronounced "Sut Nom," the vibrational meaning behind this pronunciation is to have an experience of your own consciousness. In yoga, when saying or chanting this mantra, you aim to connect to the root of your spine and go right up through the brain and into your auric field and tune in to the symphony that is your own being and the expression of truth of *all beings*. Sat Nam is less of a word or an expression as it is an experience of the true essence of you, aligning with all truth. (This definition is taken in part from Surjoy's definition of Sat Nam from www.satnamfest.com/blog/sat-nam-meaning.)

In recognizing the truth of my identity, I needed to examine not only my current life circumstances, but the ones from long ago and recognize the patterns that kept presenting themselves. And to be sure, there is more than enough in this lifetime to make me want to keep my mouth shut. I truly believe that I am one of the world's most positive people, but I think that comes from knowing how to dredge myself up out of the depths of despair and find a reason to keep going.

I read about celebrities who became wealthy and famous with themselves and their message, but had childhoods that would make you shudder (Oprah Winfrey, Maya Angelou), and I find solace and hope that every one of us can find our way out. It may not be to fame or fortune, but sanity and true joy are absolutely worth the trip.

Yoga has helped me to dig deep into essential truths about myself that I don't believe I would have found otherwise. In what I call the "yogic state," I come closest to the feelings and experiences I had when I was on the other side—a feeling of oneness with myself, with everyone else in the room, and if I'm lucky, the city, the country, and the planet. When I'm practicing and find my yogic state, the room around me ceases to exist. I usually wind up with my eyes closed and what I see or hear can be anything or nothing at all. Sometimes I can clearly see the auras of others (living or dead) or visions or insights into my own life, or those of other people. Often, things don't make sense in the moment, but later, what I saw or experienced will find its way to a more significant meaning out in the world.

When I'm teaching and find my yogic state, I speak when spoken through. This is a concept I learned about in my work with Shakti Rising. Speaking when spoken through isn't anything scary; forget what you've seen on television and movies. It simply means speaking the truth that is coming through me at that moment. I don't know where it comes from or who exactly it is, usually. It's also a mixture of how I'm feeling that day, what is present and true for me in my life, and the wisdom that comes through to me from somewhere else. Combined with yoga postures meant to strengthen and release throughout the body, it becomes an experience for the class to tap into this wisdom for themselves. It happens in a small or big way in every class I teach and in one-on-one sessions with people who ask for my help.

Recently, I reduced my teaching schedule because I noticed something happening to me in my classes. Burn-out is a word that is used often when you overdo it, but it was slightly different than that for me. Once I realized how strong the speaking when spoken through force was in my teaching, I began to seek the meaning ahead of time, and plan and structure the classes around this. When I was teaching six to eight times per week, plus occasional weekend workshops, volunteer work, my full-time job and a family, you can see how quickly this plan failed me. I realized that I was trying way too hard and was starting to lose the joy of teaching, and as a result, less messaging was coming through. My class attendance levels dipped and I was not my joyful, grounded self.

Of course, we all have good and bad days, but I knew I had to make a change. I teach a little less now and work with more private clients one-on-one and it feels a lot better. Also, what a gift for me to have more time to practice for myself now! I'll reiterate, this has been my experience. I believe it was one of the reasons I was sent back not once, not twice, but three times. For other people, finding your Nirvana so to speak, may come in the form of another activity, such as meditation (which I also incorporate daily in my personal life and classes), running, swimming, hiking, gardening or maybe just *being* in nature. You know what it is for you. Take the chance and look deeply within and at the experiences in your life that have left you feeling blissful; it has nothing to do with "checking out" and addictive socially-cultivated behaviors that we all know too well. If you are feeling like you don't know how to connect to your goodness within, try the following meditation:

> *Close your eyes, take a deep breath. Put your hand on your heart and one on your belly. As you breathe out, recall the first time you felt absolute joy. Don't judge yourself, whether you were three or forty-three, just be in what the memory is. Stay with it. Breathe in it, remember it back into your consciousness as if it is happening again right now. Let it spread throughout your body, into every little nook and cranny of your lovely self and feel at home with it being there. Cherish it. Cherish you. How does that feel?*

At what other times have you felt this feeling? If you can't think of any, keep coming back to that first memory and get used to how it feels so that you can recognize it again when it comes up again for you, because now, I promise you, it will find you and you will find it again.

Finding Your Connection

I've spent some time in my life being a semi-competitive distance runner and the infamous "runner's high" also comes close to this feeling, but to me it is more singular. The runner's high had me feeling physically and mentally insurmountable, that my stamina was unending and I could run forever. I was connected to a higher power, to be sure, and the effects of this surge caused me to no longer feel my legs or arms or even my breath. I became aware that I was a functioning being and my consciousness in a way, completely disconnected from my body, was no longer feeling the ground or my breath or my heartbeat. But I didn't feel connected to a *greater* consciousness in the way that I do in yoga. In yoga, for me, it is much different. When you start looking for your source or connection to consciousness, don't fret about what it is. Find your unique solution, the one that links the conscious action of your breath to freedom in you, in whatever way you can find it. No matter what it is, it will bring you closer to your truth.

I have a long list of life experiences, any one of which could have sent me down a very dark road at any time. If I'm to continue being authentically honest, I have had very bleak moments and periods of time that my light was so dim that it scared me. I lost both of my parents at a very young age and I then went on to endure childhood molestation, domestic violence, date-rape, and physically dying three times. It's almost funny to see all those things strung together in one sentence, because any and all of them could have been my undoing.

Again, if I'm really honest, there was also a time in my early twenties, before I had children, when my current lifetime memories of loss, violence, molestation, and rape caught up with me and I contemplated suicide. Since I had seen the other side and knew that it was so good and warm and comforting, like the best down blanket on a cold day in front of the fire, I wanted to be there. I wanted to be with my mother, I wanted to be with my great-grandparents whom I'd been fortunate to know, live with, and love when I was a child. Maybe there my father and I could actually have a conversation that mattered. The harshness of life had dragged me to the bottom of the pool and my hair was being sucked into the drain, and I wanted to be in that realm of love and never, ever leave it again. I deserved it after all, after what I'd been through. *What was the purpose of showing me how perfect death was, only to deny me entry?*

I thought about it, I gathered what I thought would be good tools to do it with, but it didn't work. If we're counting, I might have died a fourth time if I'd gone through with what I was planning, but my mother Ria came through once more and prevented me from completing what I had started – she literally would not allow me to take the action I was attempting. *A physical force made me stop.*

So what then, what does this mean to go and come back, go

and come back, go and come back? I've asked myself this question and so have the few others who know my story. I know now, that one of the reasons was to teach. Yoga is my life's work as a student, and as a teacher; it connects me back to that place over and over again. Ironically, at the end of most yoga classes we guide students into savasana, or corpse pose. People jokingly refer to this as morbid, but it has nothing to do with literal death. It's the death of the ego. Each time we do yoga, theoretically, we are lying down to rest or die each time, and then we rise up again, fresh, ready to start again and again and again. In real life we all die little (or big) deaths over and over and over again.

In varying degrees, we die a little or a lot everyday. Think about that. Every harsh criticism others cast out on us, or that we believe about ourselves. Anytime anyone ever said a mean thing to you or that you said to yourself. Anytime you went through a really bad break-up and it felt like you really were dying. So many deaths, and, so many chances to start again. How do you respond to these periods in the deep?

Recall briefly, your first broken heart. Was it a romantic relationship or something else? For example, I have chronic lumbar (lower) and thoracic (mid-upper) spinal pain. My low back has discs that are completely compressed and also a slight S curvature, so the x-rays explain that pain and a regimen of yoga and occasional chiropractic and acupuncture adjustments help me tremendously. But what about the upper back? After practicing yoga for years and getting regular chiropractic care, my current chiropractor asked me about my heart.

What?

She asked me, when my heart had been broken, was I nursing an old wound, because something was living in and blocking my heart. I chuckled and said sure, I'd had some heartbreak in my teenage years, but I'd met my husband young; I really didn't feel that to be accurate for me. She probed some more and asked me about significant losses in my life. Had anyone major in my life passed away when I was young. Sure, my great-grandparents, but that was expected, they were in their 80s and 90s. My aunt Caroline, too, had passed when I was young and that had been devastating. Since I couldn't seem to recall the obvious, she looked at my new patient intake notes.

"Both your parents died when you were little?" she asked.

"Yes," I responded, "but I can barely remember my dad and I don't remember my mom at all."

She just looked at me. Then it sunk in and I told her about how after my mom had her accident and was in the hospital in a coma, I had apparently cried for three days, non-stop. I didn't sleep or eat. No one could console me. No one knew what to do with me. Different family members and friends came but the result was the same. Finally, my mother's mother, the woman who eventually raised me, came and picked me up, and so I've been told I immediately calmed, put my head on her shoulder, and fell asleep. When my mother died a few days later, the decision was made for me to return to Canada with my grandmother on a temporary basis until my dad could get back on his feet.

Could this be the cause of my physical pain, manifesting in my body in the only way that would eventually get me to listen? This is the second reason the trip to the afterlife or whatever you want to call it, reached out to me—to bring something back that has healing embedded within it, for all of us. *When there is no medically-sourced diagnosis for our pain, we must turn inward.*

Emotions have the ability to affect our physicality, just as physical pain manifests intense emotions and agony; we don't question that. Years of physical pain bring a measurable toll not just to the body, but to the mind and the spirit. I think most of us accept this as common sense: When you are worn down physically, eventually the spirit suffers. Well-meaning people visit you in home or in hospice and encourage you to keep your chin up because we all know how much physical limitation makes us feel caged in and can wear down the mind and even the most jubilant attitude. But look at it the other way, too. Everything from minor to major pain in the absence of a provable medical condition also has an explanation; we are often just reluctant to do this work, because let's face it, it hurts too much and there's no easy prescription to make it go away.

I made a trip back to Bermuda, where I had been born when Richard and I got married in 1996 and again in 2008. On that second trip, I spoke to one of my uncles about the man who had been driving the firetruck that had killed my mother. His name was Victor. Through the recounting of the story from my family and from a couple of days spent at the library viewing microfiche files from the newspaper, I was able to put together the last days of my mother's life.

July 1974, Hamilton, Bermuda

On July 2, 1974, my mother left home for her job as a waitress at a high-end hotel in a wealthy area of the island. I was six months old and was at home with a trusted friend and caregiver named Margaret. My father also had a job requiring he work evenings as a bar manager in another establishment. My mother rode a moped to and from work and had pulled up to a stoplight at an intersection at the bottom of a hill. As she crossed the intersection when the light turned green, she was struck directly by a firetruck that barreled through the intersection because the brakes had failed while it was out on a test run. My mother, her scooter, and the fire truck flew off the edge of a cliff just beyond the intersection and landed on the beach below.

Incredibly, everyone involved survived the initial impact. The drivers of the truck initially did not realize that they had hit a person as they were so caught up in the crash and the brakes failing, but they were able to walk away from the scene. Hours later, when a crane lifted the truck up off the beach, they were horrified to discover my mother underneath. In the ensuing week, my mother had one of her arms amputated as it was crushed beyond repair. When my grandmother arrived from Canada, she was not prepared for what she saw: a completely unrecognizable and swollen daughter who was comatose and missing a limb. Ria's lungs were collapsing and continuously filling with fluid, and although she remained unconscious, she stayed alive for just over a week. My grandmother tells me that she talked to Ria every day, telling her to hang on, that she would get better, that she had a baby and a family and so much to hang on for. I believe my mother did just that—hung on.

The doctors eventually had to tell my grandmother that things were not going well and she needed to prepare herself to say goodbye. My mother's injuries were far too severe to recover from. My grandmother did not want to submit to this conclusion and at first, refused. However, she eventually returned to my mother's bedside and calmly told her that she could let go, that she would take care of me, that everything would be okay, that if the pain was too much and it was time to go, then, go. My grandmother says that in that moment my mother's eyes fluttered open, the machines attached to her recognized an uptick in brain and bodily activity, and my mother's mouth started moving as a tear ran down her face. My grandmother rushed out of the room to get help, convinced that my mother was coming back. But it was not to be so and Maria Monica Van Brabant [Mrs. Maria (Ria) Paynter] died on July 10, 1974 at the age of twenty-three.

When I found the newspaper articles detailing the accident, the drivers and the trial that happened years later (that resulted in no charges), I told my uncles that I wanted to meet the man who had been driving the truck. Apparently, he was a friend of my mother's and at one point had supposedly confessed feelings for her that she did not reciprocate. He had been drinking alcohol that night and was a volunteer firefighter called in at the last moment to test out a new truck. At the trial, the news articles stated that the other man in the firetruck noticed warning lights coming up on the dashboard before they got to the hill where the accident with my mother occurred and that he had advised they turn around and go back. Victor, though, did not listen to that advice and it remains unknown whether alcohol, emotion or overall poor judgement resulted in what came next.

My uncle said it was not a good idea to see Victor, as revenge or anger wasn't necessary nor good to stir up all these years later. I let him know that I just wanted to lay eyes on him. I wanted to see the man who had done this and maybe exchange a few words with him. It wasn't out of anger, I just wanted some sort of closure and I felt this might be it. I had no intention of leveling any kind of acrimony towards him. My uncle became choked up and told me it wasn't possible to see Victor. I asked him why and learned that Victor had taken his own life only a few years earlier. While he was never convicted at a legal trial and did not serve jail time, he was convicted by the court of public opinion.

Apparently, Victor hung himself after a lifetime of judgment and suspicion from the entire community. I wasn't sure in learning about this what hurt more; there were so many layers of loss and pain! Amazingly, I felt instant compassion and love for this man, who apparently might have loved my mother and died never being loved by another.

So this is another lesson I believe that I bring back: Holding onto anger, even when everyone and everything in the world tells you it's justified, only hurts you. Forgiveness helps you more than you would ever believe possible and true forgiveness comes from being able to feel true connection and compassion to another being, even when they have hurt you. I'm not a licensed therapist and am not looking to be one, and I in no way want to gloss over people's pain and sense of justice. BUT, if you are unable to find a path to compassion and forgiveness, you will be unable to heal the part that is hurting. Sometimes, oftentimes actually, it is yourself you need to forgive more than any other. This is the hardest work of all because we are most ferocious with our own selves. We say and do things to our psyche, our body, and our spirit that we would never say to or wish upon a worst enemy; it's really hard to spot the dragons sometimes.

When I held onto that pain of losing my mother, I believe that it manifested into serious back pain forty years later. I'd long since thought that I'd gotten over the effects of her death, but I was wrong. I had sealed it up tight and formed a barbed wire fence around it to be sure that I and no one else could find it. What other kinds of love had I been shutting out of my life because of that defense mechanism? What about the anger that goes with a broken heart? For all the yoga I'd been doing and even my steady chiropractic appointments, I had buried deep a boiling, festering wound that I was determined to hold onto. I had to forgive myself for holding onto that baggage of hurt and I had to forgive everyone and everything associated with that accident.

But, what about Victor? Unrequited love and a bad combination of drinking and driving resulted in the death of the woman he had feelings for, and when she died, he never went to jail. I don't know a lot about how the law works, but I know enough that in 1974 they didn't have the measures in place to convict people of DUIs like they do now. However, from what I've gleaned, Victor suffered a far worse type of imprisonment than the legal system could have imposed. It is physically painful for me to close my eyes and think about what led to Victor taking his own life, the same pain I feel if I close my eyes and think about the crane pulling that truck up off of my mother on the beach.

An eye for an eye does not feel good to me… it truly feels downright awful.

Chapter Ten
Gayatri

March 1986, in the American South

When I was twelve, my grandparents and I drove from southern Ontario, Canada down to Disney World in Orlando, Florida for my winter break from school. I was excited to go. I was excited for sunshine, for going on rides, to be able to swim and to get away. The ride there was unremarkable. We drove almost straight through, staying with a family friend overnight who lived in a northern part of Florida. The really disturbing memories are from our trip back home.

It started at a restaurant in Georgia where we had stopped for lunch. They told us they didn't have any tables available and we would have to wait. We watched as they sat table after table of other families, but not us. My grandfather became irritated and asked why everyone else was being seated, but not us. We had requested non-smoking and were finally seated—in the middle of the smoking section. I thought that was extremely odd and I didn't want to stay. I could feel and see all the eyes of those in the restaurant looking at me and they weren't smiling. *What was going on?*

I stood up and asked our waitress where the restrooms were.

She replied that they were out of order. I sat back down. My grandfather got up and went to find the restrooms, and it turned out they were not out of order; he pointed me in the direction of them. When I got there, two big burly men blocked my entrance to the restroom and so I returned to the table, frightened.

When our lunch came, the waitress slammed my drink on the table, spilling at least the top third of it. She glared at me and did not apologize. My grandfather, in a low growly voice said, "Hey there, watch it now," to her and she ignored him and walked away. The food was not what I had ordered and looked sloppy. I didn't want to eat it. I asked my grandparents what was happening; why was everyone being so mean to us? My grandmother explained that with my "tan" from being out in the sun and my short curly hair, my black heritage was clear as day to everyone in the restaurant and that we were in a part of the country that didn't like black people. I was stunned and mortified and wanted to leave immediately. I'd had my share of name-calling and minor bullying at my pretty much all-white school from time to time, but this was something else entirely. I picked at my food because I didn't want to be wasteful, but it was awful.

Within a couple of hours of being back on the road, my body began to feel the effects of whatever they had done to the food as my stomach rejected it over and over again. Intense vomiting and diarrhea meant we had to stop often and then, if the attendant saw me, sometimes they wouldn't let my grandfather pump gas or allow me to use the restroom. We had to keep me lying low in the back of the car while he pulled up and then drive around the side to the restroom so that hopefully, they wouldn't see me. Sometimes, we had to stop on the side of the road. It was physical and emotional torture and I remember thinking I was going to die. By the end of the day, I had developed a raging fever and was lying down in the backseat of our car, shivering and unable to talk.

The tipping point came the next day, when I was starting to feel a bit better and we pulled up into a small town in Tennessee. My grandparents wanted to look at an antique market and said they would drop me off on the main street not too far away in town to look at stores and books instead if I wanted. I had a little bit of spending money and I looked forward to it. I wandered into a diner and the waitress was sweet and got me a coke and I sat at the bar and enjoyed it. As I left the diner, I noticed a sheriff-type looking guy get up from his seat and follow me out. I next went into a pharmacy and bought a Bonnie Bell Lip Smacker Rollerball lip gloss, in cherry flavor. I was excited about that. It smelled good and tasted good and all the girls in my grade wore it. My lips were chapped and sunburned from a sad combination of being sick and swimming for hours at the hotel pool. The lady working behind the counter there was sweet to me too and she waved and smiled and said, "Hey there,

Harv" to the sheriff-looking man who had come inside as well.

I felt a little weird leaving and seeing him stand by the door, very close to me, just staring at me as I walked past him. Next, I went into a clothing store and there a nice lady said hello to me and asked if I needed any help. I explained I was just waiting for my grandparents, who were up the road and I was trying to keep busy. Harv came in this store after me as well and stood there, glaring. I was beginning to feel alarmed and I looked at the saleslady in fear. She shook her head and patted my hand and called out, "Hey Harv, you be nice now, you hear?"

I continued walking up the street and decided to head all the way back up towards the antique barn and find my grandparents. I didn't feel safe. Harv walked behind me the whole time. He was talking, muttering really, but I couldn't hear him clearly and so I walked as fast as I could. My stomach was still weak and my spirit was weary, too. I was afraid and yet I moved those feet as fast as I could without running. Because part of the walk was through woods and a bit of a dirt road, I became more fearful as I lost the presence of other eyes and businesses around us. As soon as I could see the barn, I did start to run and much to my horror, Harv did, too.

I breathlessly came upon my grandparents in negotiation with the antique dealer and was trying to talk when Harv came right up, red-faced and sweating and screaming, at the top of his lungs: "Next time y'all come out here you keep that thing on a LEASH!" as he pointed, but did not look, directly at me. He was heaving and huffing and puffing, and I think I fell down on the ground. It felt like the wind had been knocked out of me and I had been physically punched.

My grandfather roared to life, immediately striding towards Harv, arms raised and ready to fight. My grandmother came over to me right away and started half-dragging me towards the car. She told me to get in it and get down and lock the doors. She got in with me, too. I don't know what happened between Harv and my grandfather. I think the antique shop owner might have intervened to keep them apart because within a few moments, during which I swear I held my breath the whole time, he was back in the car and we kept driving until we got back to Canada. We stopped for gas where we could, but as we got farther and farther north, this became less of a problem.

I share this here now because this was a type of death for me. I suspect it was for my grandfather, too. As a white man raising his mixed-race grandchild, who was not even biologically related to him, and of whom he didn't approve of initially but had grown to love and protect, I can only imagine how his heart had burst. I can only imagine how frightened and mad he was. If they had come to blows, what consequences might have come of that? I shudder to think. He took the next right action in getting us all out of there as quickly as possible.

No more lingering, no more pretending everything was okay when it was clearly not. I also share this because it was the first time I experienced a hatred toward me that I fully realized actually had *nothing to do with me.* I remember saying to my grandmother that it made no sense. How could someone hate someone else that they did not know? She explained that it was hatred of all black people and that it didn't matter who I was as a person. I couldn't grasp it, but my young mind knew instinctually that this was very, very wrong. How could so many people feel this way?

You can call it naive, but I call it truth. All of us know these truths. How it shows up in our lives and experiences will always be different, but the proof is there. Go back to the first time you knew something that had happened or was said that was really wrong, whether it had to do with you or someone else. Remember that feeling? You do. Did someone else quash it? Did you? This is not a blame game. This is more like hide and seek. Connect to those feelings and don't ignore them when it rears up in your life.

We did not speak of this particular incident again in our family, but I wish we had. I wrote about it in my journal, but I didn't tell friends or other family. I immediately took the blame for the incident. If only I hadn't been there. If only I'd just stayed with my grandparents in the barn instead of wanting to go out on my own. If only. I did the most damage to myself by choosing to push down the knowing what was right and wrong about the situation and by choosing to feel bad about who I was.

The last time I saw my grandfather in physical form was about two weeks before I moved to California. He had been checked into the hospital again for recurring pneumonia. He was ninety-one. I knew, we both knew somehow, that this would be the last time we would see each other. I broke down. I apologized for all the trouble I had ever brought him. I apologized for the times I was a jerk when I was a teenager. I apologized for not telling him more often what a good dad he had been to me in my own biological father's stead. And you know what? He just looked at me and smiled a huge smile and said, "I don't know what you're talking about, Megan. You have brought nothing but joy to my life. That other stuff? It never even mattered. I love you. You've always been my sweetheart."

A little over a year after we moved to California, just as I had re-applied for my passport in preparation for a trip home, I received word that he was back in the hospital and it was looking bad. Sepsis had taken over his body. In a panic, I looked into contacting the embassy and the Canadian government to see if I could travel without my passport and to explain the situation. It was evening. My uncle Guy explained to me that I would never make it in time; he wasn't expected to last the night. I cried and cried and cried.

I sang the Gayatri Mantra over and over again. When I would begin to emotionally choke on the sounds I would listen to the Tina Malia version instead. The Gayatri Mantra is said to heal all wounds and bring lightness to all those who chant or even hear it. I dreamt of my grandfather that night, watching him pass over into eternal sweetness, enmeshed in light and warmth. He was smiling. He was free.

>Om bhur bhuvah svaha
>tat savitur varenyam
>bargo devasya dhimahi
>dhiyo yonah prachodayat

"Let us honor the unity of Divine Spirit that
pervades all realms of existence:
the earth, the atmosphere and the heavens.
May that most brilliant Divine Light protect us,
sustain us and illuminate our consciousness
That we might realize our inherent goodness,
our inborn divinity and our unity with All That Is.
By this knowledge may our actions be inspired."

The above translation courtesy of:
http://www.discoveryyoga.com/Gayatri%20Mantra.htm

Outro

Our stories are never really finished. I struggled when writing this book to come up with the appropriate ending. I mean, isn't the conclusion of a book supposed to be where everything is tied up neatly together and everyone feels good and you've come away with "the answer?" In Hollywood stories maybe, but not in real life usually. Could I, dare I, talk about finding ways to help even just one other person to find their own magnificent revelation of compassion, communion with higher self, and forgiveness? That's a tall order, but I hope this book is that starting point for at least a few of you. That is my honest wish.

In writing and sharing our stories, the end goal, I believe, is to turn the reader's personal blend of Vitamix chaos into some sort of order and craft a message, *your message* from that mess. So, what comes after that then, is doing the next right thing. The right thing for you, I mean. Each time we are faced with a conundrum we have to ask ourselves: What is right for me? What is right for others? What is right for this situation? Right now. Not tomorrow, or next week or next year, not what your mom said seventeen years ago or what your uncle said is most appropriate, but right now. This approach can get us safely and lovingly out of almost any situation.

My grandmother just celebrated her ninety-second birthday. While still alive, she has noticeably slowed down now, and as she was born just before World War II, her life has seen the arc of so many incredible things. She doesn't understand the concept of the internet or Wi-Fi, and when I showed her how a laptop computer could show a picture of the church in her hometown in Belgium, she was at first delighted and then she became totally terrified. She's had several brushes with death in the last ten years or so, including bouts of cancer, mini strokes, heart attacks, falls, and severe flu episodes. In some of these instances, I have dreamt it and met her in the in-between spaces and woke up to find out she was in the hospital.

In one of my conversations with her, she talked about meeting and approaching death. She could feel herself slipping away. She talked about feeling good, letting go, and feeling warm and cozy. She saw Ria and they talked. I saw this moment, too, in my dream. But then, in the back of her mind, she still had not been ready to go and she held back. Her lingering thought at the time was: *"I wish I'd had more time to figure out the end of me."*

When I asked her to explain that, she had a hard time. She talked about funeral arrangements, her will, her belongings, how all of that was set up so that we, her kids and family, would not have to worry about it when she's gone.

"So what is it then?" I asked her again.

She said that it was hard for her to understand what the end of her life actually meant. She is a raised and practicing devout Catholic, she's adhered to the principles taught to her by the church as best she can and for as long as she can remember, and she has always trusted in what she was told about life and death. But she's feeling less sure about all that now. She's not feeling done with her life, with herself, with her concept of self, of "me." Her life had always been about surviving first, then raising a family. Continuously building, sewing, cooking, renovating, always going, going, going. She never had a long-term career, though for a time she worked as the head sewing consultant for Sears in the 1950s.

Now, though, she spends so much time alone and she can't move very fast, nor can she see or hear very well. She spends hours a day in prayer and meditation. She can only live literally from moment to moment and this is a new experience for her. As someone who, throughout her life has worried and fretted about the countless "what ifs" of the future on a constant loop and repeat in her mind, this is quite a return to stasis. She physically wants to go on and has prepared herself above and beyond to do so in the literal and logical sense. Her "me," though, still has something to teach her it seems.

In the end then, the return to life (from death), the return to self (either through metaphorical or actual death), the "me" of all this keeps bringing us back to where we need to be at any moment. It offers up what our next right thing is, it shows up in ways that we don't expect, and most of all, it wants us to find it. For some of us, these realizations may not start really percolating until we've reached nearly a century of life, and for others, the awareness starts very soon after birth. On this first day of my forty-fourth year, I am finalizing these last words of what I want to share with you about the End of Me…

I believe in the power and tradition of storytelling. By telling our stories we give others permission to tell theirs too and provide the opportunity to find and further human connection.

At any moment the essence, birth, and death of the "me" is waiting to be called out, to be able to show up for you, to emerge and shine forth. It is in our true recognizing and welcoming of this old friend and then in choosing to share it first within ourselves to make it real again that allows us to begin to navigate with it back out into the physical world. It is there to be found by everyone, so that they, too, can find their own sweet return to life and to death, for they are both really one and the same thing.

Resources

These are some of the people and organizations that have played a large part in my training, experiences, and support system. You may find them helpful both in person or even at a distance, if you don't live in these cities.

Shakti Rising
Dedicated to the empowerment and enrichment of women and girls everywhere and the men who support them:
https://www.shaktirising.org

Magdalen University
Psychic School, Counseling and Energy Healing:
https://www.aureyamagdalen.life

Real, Authentic, Wild
This is the yoga studio I teach at, which offers a plethora of classes, teaching styles, and workshops:
http://www.realauthenticwild.com

Ayurvedic Nutrition
My friend, Sandra, is an Ayurvedic Doctor and yoga teacher. She introduced me to Shakti Rising:
http://www.sandragutierrez.org

Oracle Reading

Halley is an oracle reader, intuitive healer, and energy worker. We went to Psychic School together!
http://halleymiglietta.com

Teacher Training

IGita is where I did my first yoga teacher certification in Canada:
http://www.omlife.ca

Basic Family Tree

Unknown	Charles Segers
&	&
Unknown	Flavia Craeye

Percival Paynter	Joseph Van Brabant
&	&
Ruth Williamson	Madeline Segers
	Madeline remarries:
	Chester Dodds

| Ronald Paynter | Maria Van Brabant |

Megan Morgan